THE DISK
FROM PHAISTOS

Victor J. Kean

The DISK from PHAISTOS

ISBN 960 226 099 8

Reprinted 1990

Photography by K. Kolatsoglou

Distributed by:
EFSTATHIADIS GROUP S.A.
Ag. Athanasiou Str. GR. 145 65 Anixi Attikis Tel. 8136871-2
14 Valtetsiou St. GR 106 80 Athens Tel. 3615011
34 Olympou-Diikitiriou St. GR. 546 30 Thessaloniki Tel. 511781

EFSTATHIADIS GROUP
Bookshop: 84 Academias St. Tel. 3637439

To my dear friend Sybille C. Beyer for her help
and encouragement.

The Author wishes to acknowledge
the advice freely given
by Professor Dr. J. A. Sakellarakis of
the Heraklion Museum, Crete.

CONTENTS

1. Foreword   9

2. Description   11

3. Table of Symbols   17

4. Steps to Decipherment   22

5. The Forty-five Symbols   30

6. Tables of Frequency   66

7. The Sixty-one Phrases   72

8. Legend of the Disk   110

9. Summary   116

10. Bibliography   119

11. **Captions**   **121**

PALACE OF PHAISTOS

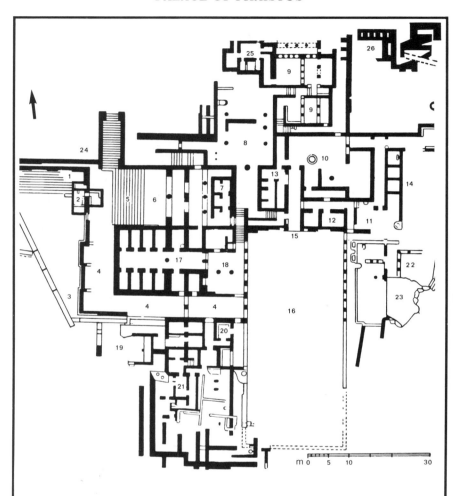

1. West Court or Theatrical Area
2. A shrine complex of the first palace
3. West Façade of the first palace
4. Corridor
5. Grand staircase
6. Propylaion
7. Magazines of the First palace with pithoi
8. Peristyle hall
9. Queen's apartment
10. Internal Court
11. Artisan's Rooms
12. Rooms with earlier Peristyle
13. Rooms with Hermaria
14. Workshops
15. Central Court Corridor
16. Central Court
17. Double line of Magazines
18. Pillared hall
19. Sanctuaries of the West Wing
20. Rooms with benches
21. Southwest Pillar and rooms
22. Portico with Columns on two sides
23. Probably Workshops
24. Hellenistic building Including an Exedra
25. Lustral basin
26. A complex of Rooms from one of them
    came the famous Phaistos Disk.

1. Foreword

The first time I visited the island of Crete it was to enjoy the wonders of the Minoan palaces at Knossos, Malia and Phaistos. It was at the last of these that I first heard of the artifact that commands so much attention at the museum at Heraklion .... The Phaistos Disk.

Over the next three years I read many learned works about this unique item and its tiny inscriptions whose meaning had eluded the many experts who had tried to explain them.

My own initial efforts were frustrating and quite disheartening for the feeling of initial familiarity with the symbols seemed to disappear the more one studied them.

It was the reading of the words of Cyrus H. Gordon in his book "Forgotten Scripts" that filled me with fresh resolve. "When any person takes the first and critical steps to transform a category of mysterious inscriptions into intelligible documents by revealing their script or language we shall call the achievement a decipherment."

I now submit to my reader's scrutiny my efforts to unlock this ancient mystery.

Victor J. Kean.

2. Description

The Disk from Phaistos is a round plate of terra-cotta having a diameter of 16cms. (6 ins.). It is approx. 2cms. thick.

On both faces of the Disk are a mixture of pictograms and ideograms printed in a spiral form in a sequence of phrases. The phrases vary in the number of symbols of which they are composed.

The Disk was unearthed in 1908 by Doctor L. Pernier, member of the Italian archaeological mission led by Prof. F. Halberr. It was found in the first of a number of narrow, stone-lined cysts in the Old Palace. These small chambers were apparently used for the storage of precious objects. The Disk was dated as being pre - 1600 B.C. by the undisputed age of the Linear A tablets found in the earth surrounding it.

Each of the forty-five symbols has been printed into the clay whilst it was still wet by the use of individual dies. Each ot these dies was between 6mm. and 16mm. high. Carved with precise details they were probably made of wood.

Many of the experts who have examined the Disk believe that it was accidentally hardened by a raging fire which followed a series of earthquakes which destroyed the Old palace. I find this view difficult to accept. Whoever had the skill to produce the Disk surely had the knowledge as to how to preserve it.

The Palace of Phaistos stands some 5kms. inland from the southern coast of the Island of Crete on a mountain range overlooking the fertile Messara plain.

Whilst many opinions have been expressed as to the contents of the Phaistos Disk and of its origins none have been generally accepted.

One of the first persons to have an opportunity to study the Disk was (Sir) Arthur Evans who was working at Knossos at the time of its discovery. He concluded that it was a hymn to the Earth Goddess. [1]

Other opinions have included, "A Hymn to the Rain God in Basque" ..... "A Hymn to Rhea in Greek" ...... "A Hymn of Victory the whole being the text of a sacred song" ...... "A list of thirteen soldier's names".

Following the decipherment of the Linear B script in 1952 by Michael Ventris in collaboration with Chadwick, which established that Linear B was an archaic form of Greek [2], attempts have also been made to allot phonetic values to the symbols of the Phaistos Disk and thereby prove that it is a "continuance of the Minoan language". [3] Apart from general agreement that the Disk either originated in Crete or arrived at that island along one of the known trade routes, its origins have been variously attributed to Anatolia, Libya or Cyprus and its contents thought to be Philistine, Carian, Semitic, Lycian etc. ......

1 Palace of Minos   Arthur Evans   1921-35
2 Greek records in the Minoan Script   Michael Ventris   1953
3 Evidence for the Minoan Language   Cyrus H. Gordon   1972

Front Face

The Disk from Phaistos is on display in Case 41 in Room III of the Heraklion Museum, Crete.

Rear Face

KRITIKO PELAGOS

KP

KR

Andikithira
Αντικύθηρα

To Gythion

Akr. Spanda
Akr. Σπάντα

Kolpos Hanion
Κόλπος Χανίω

Kolpos Kissamou

Radopou
Ροδοπού

Akr. Tripiti
Akr. Τρίπητη

Moni Ag. Ioannou
Μονή Αγ. Ιωάννου

To Piraeus

Seronikos
Γερόνικος

Ag. Georgios
Αγ. Γεώργιος

Kastell
Καστέλι

Ravdoula
Ραβδούχα

Kolimvari
Κολυμβάρι

Koumares
Κουμαρές

Platanos
Πλάτανος

Drapania

Tavronitis

43

Agia Marina
Αγία Μαρίνα

Hania
Χανιά

Souda

Kounoupidi

Rizoklima

Palimilia

Rokka
Ρόκκα

Episkopi
Επισκοπή

Meleme
Μέλεμε

Platanias
Πλατανιάς

Mournies
Μουρνιές

Akr. Drapano
Akr. Δράπανο

Slinara
Σλίναρα

Topolis
Τοπόλις

Zimbragou
Ζυμπράγου

Oreas
Ωρέας

Skonizo
Σκονιζό

Fournes
Φουρνές

Panagia
Παναγιά

Maleza
Μαλέζα

Plaka
Πλάκα

Kefalas
Κεφαλάς

Kambos
Κάμπος

Elos
Έλος

Strovles
Στρόβλες

Floria
Φλωριά

Palea Roumata

Orthouni
Ορθούνι

Theriso
Θέρισο

Drakona
Δράκονα

Kambi
Κάμπι

Vamos
Βάμος

Moni Hrisoskalitissas
Μονή Χρυσοσκαλίτισσας

Voutas
Βουτάς

Kandanos
Κάντανος

Epanohori
Επανοχώρι

Omalos
Ομαλός

Lakki
Λάκκι

Zourva
Ζούρβα

Prases
Πράσες

Tzitzifes
Τζιτζιφές

Georgioupoli
Γεωργιούπολη

Ormos Almirou
Ορμος Αλμιρού

63

Kriti
Κρ

Rethimno
Ρέθυμνο

Kaprodiki
Καπροδίκη

Temenia
Τεμένια

Rodovani
Ροδοβάνι

Samaria Samaria

Lefka Ori
Λευκά Όρη

Embrosneros
Εμπροσνερος

Vrises
Βρύσες

Alikambos
Αλικαμπος

Vafes
Βαφές

Dramia

Gerani
Γερανι

Doliana
Δολιανά

Geni
Γενή

Atsipopoulo

Argiroupoli
Αργυρούπολη

Roustika

Skouloufia

Margarites

Perama
Πέραμα

Akr. Krios
Akr. Κριός

Palechora
Παλαιοχώρα

Sougia
Σούγια

Koustogerako
Κουστογέρακο

Agia Roumeli
Αγία Ρούμελη

Azogiria
Αζωγυρά

Asfendou
Ασφένδου

Miriokefala
Μυριοκέφαλα

Kourna
Κούρνα

Moni Arkadiou
Μονή Αρκαδίου

Eleftherna
Ελεύθερνα

Kalikratis
Καλλικράτης

Rodakini
Ροδάκινι

Karines
Καρινές

Patsos
Πάτσος

Apostoli
Απόστολι

Spili
Σπήλι

Moni Asomaton
Μονή Ασωμάτων

Anopoli
Ανώπολη

Sfakia
Σφακιά

Patsianos
Πατσιανός

Skaloti
Σκαλωτή

Sellia
Σελλιά

Plakias
Πλακιάς

Mariou
Μαρίου

Amari
Αμάρι

Fourfouras
Φουρφουράς

Piso Moni Preveli
Πίσω Μονή Πρέβελη

Kotsifou
Κοτσιφού

Kerames
Κεραμές

Akoumia
Ακούμια

Ano Meros
Άνω Μέρος

53

Nithavris
Νίθαυρις

Platanos
Πλάτανος

Melambes
Μελάμπες

Agia Galini
Αγία Γαλήνη

Klima
Κλήμα

Akr. Melissa
Akr. Μέλισσα

Timbaki

Ag. Triada

Gavdopoula
Γαυδοπούλα

Paximadia
Παξιμάδια

Ormos Mesaras
Ορμος Μεσαράς

PHA

Mátala

Ambelos
Αμπελος

Gavdos
Γαύδος

Kastri
Καστρί

Moni Odigitrias
Μονή Οδηγήτριας

Akr. Lithino
Akr. Λίθινο

Kali Limenes
Καλοί Λιμένες

Vatsiana
Βατσιανά

LIVIKO PELAGOS

ΛΙΒΥΚ

© FREYTAG-BERNDT u. ARTARIA, WIEN

14

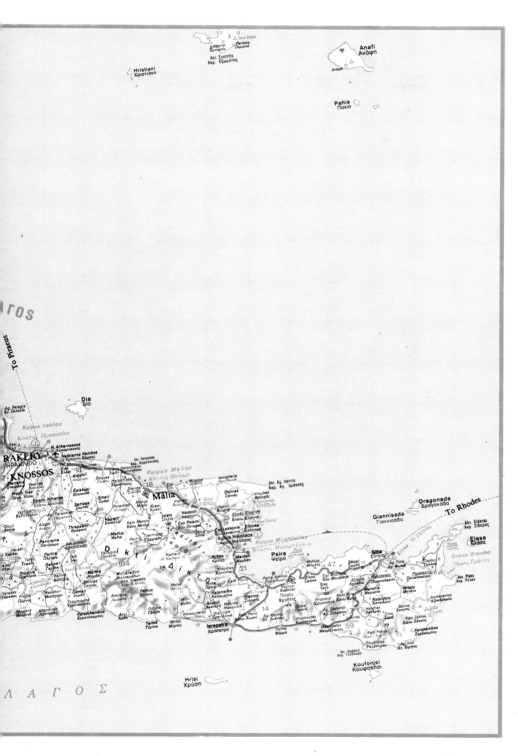

Hristiani
Χριστιάνη

Emborio
Εμπορειό
Akr. Exomitis
Ακρ. Εξωμύτης

Thira Θήρα
Perissa
Περίσσα

Anafi
Ανάφη

Anafi
Ανάφη

Pahia
Παχιά

To Piraeus

ros

Dia
Δία

Ag. Pelagia
Αγ. Πελαγία
Kolpos Irakliou
Κόλπος Ηρακλείου
Gazi

N. Alikarnassos
Ν. Αλικαρνασσός
RAKLIO
ΗΡΑΚΛΕΙΟ
KNOSSOS

Vathianos Kambos
Βαθιανός Κάμπος
Akr. Hersonisou
Ακρ. Χερσονήσου
Hersonisos
Χερσόνησος
Kolpos Malion
Κόλπος Μαλίων

Amigdala
Αμυγδαλα

Akr. Ag. Ioannis
Ακρ. Αγ. Ιωάννης

Dragonada
Δραγονάδα
To Rhodes

Giannisada
Γιαννισάδα

Akr. Sideros
Ακρ. Σίδερος

Elasa
Έλασα

Ormos Grandes
Όρμος Γράντες

Akr. Plaka
Ακρ. Πλάκα

Sitia
Σητεία

Psira
Ψείρα

Agios Nikolaos
Άγιος Νικόλαος
Kolpos Mirambellou
Κόλπος Μιραμπέλλου

Kritsa
Κριτσά

Ierapetra
Ιεράπετρα

Koufonisi
Κουφονήσι

Hrisi
Χρύση

ΛΑΓΟΣ

15

Throughout the Disk an Egyptian influence is apparent as there is in much Minoan Art.[1] This is understandable since the Messara region in Crete which is overlooked by the Palace of Phaistos was the earliest part of Crete to show Egyptian influences.[2]

It has been established that as early as 2500 B.C. Egyptian stone vases were imported into Crete and imitated by Cretan craftsmen.[3]

From my studies of the Phaistos Disk it is my opinion that the Disk is Minoan and was probably made in the period known as Middle Minoan I (2100-1900 B.C.)

As to the contents, it is the story of one man's adventures or, to be more precise, part of the story; unfortunately for us the story remains unfinished.

Of course, certainty is not claimed, and until other artifacts bearing similar symbols are unearthed, no possible decipherment can be proved.

It has been suggested that a Double-Axe from the cave sanctuary of Arkalachori in Crete which is now on display in Case 98; Room VII of the Heraklion Museum bears similar markings to those found on the Disk. (See Fig. 1)

The possibility that sometime in the future similarly inscribed Disks may be recovered always remains, since the work of the Italian archaeologists at Phaistos continues each season.

Much has been written elsewhere on the significance of the spiral form and of its possible magical connotations.[4]

Spiral and spiral-based designs developed in the Aegean before 2500 B.C.[5] Consecutive spirals running in opposite directions form a favourite decorative theme in Cretan Art.

As used on the Phaistos Disk, the spiral form would seem to emphasise the passing of time as the legend unfolds.

Fig. 1

1 Minoan and Mycenaean Art.		Pg. 18	Reynold Higgins	1967
2 End of Atlantis.	Pg. 131	J.V. Luce	1969	
3 End of Atlantis.	Pg. 134	J.V. Luce	1969	
4 Prehistoric and Ancient Art		Pg. 170	Rene Huyghe	1981
5 The Arts in Prehistoric Greece		Pg. 234	Sinclair Hood	1978

3. Table of Symbols

It is generally accepted that the face of the Disk with the eight-petalled Rosette at its centre is the FRONT face. The Disk is displayed by the Heraklion Museum in this way and certainly there is an aesthetic appearance about the centre decoration on this side that does not exist on the reverse.

It has also been established that the Disk is to be read from the centre to the outside rim.* Credit for this goes to H.D. Ephron who on purely objective and mechanical grounds determined that the direction of the script was from left-to-right. This left-to-right direction is also emphasised by the direction in which all the human symbols face; and is further collaborated by the crowding together of the symbols to the right between the phrase dividers.

No.	Symbol	No.	Symbol	No.	Symbol	No.	Symbol	No.	Symbol
1		10		19		28		37	
2		11		20		29		38	
3		12		21		30		39	
4		13		22		31		40	
5		14		23		32		41	
6		15		24		33		42	
7		16		25		34		43	
8		17		26		35		44	
9		18		27		36		45	

Each symbol has been given a SYMBOL NUMBER in the order in which they appear on the Disk, commencing with the Eight-petalled Rosette in the centre of the front face.

* Hygieia Tharso and Iaon: The Phaistos Disk   H.D. Ephron   1962

4. Steps to Decipherment

Having given each of the symbols an individual number starting from the front face (Table No. 1) the phrases were also numbered in a similar fashion.

Phrases Nos. 1-31 being on the front face and Phrases Nos. 32-61 being on the rear face.

The two sides of the Disk are listed out in numerical form (Tables 2 and 3). In this way repetitive patterns and sequences are more easily seen.

The frequency of occurence of the individual symbols is shown in Table 4 and the existence of Pairs, Triples and larger groups is tabulated in Table 5.

The occurence of like pairs is shown in Table 6 and an attempt at grouping in general terms is made in Table 7.

Studies of these various tables revealed that the subject matter of the Disk was concerned primarily with six particular symbols.

These are Symbols   No. 4 Striding Man
No. 9 Animal's Hide
No. 10 Seven Dots (Encl)
No. 11 Man with Headdress
No. 17 Direction Sign
and No. 26 Water Container

Together these six symbols account for 92 of the 241 legible impressions. This is 38% of the total.

The pairing together of Symbols Nos. 10 and 11 on thirteen occasions accounts for a quarter of the subject matter.

TABLE No. 2

Front Face

Phrase No.	Symbol Numbers
1	1 : 2 : 3
2	4 : 5
3	6 : 7 : 8 : 9 : 9 : 10 : 11
4	1 : 2 : 3
5	8 : 12 : 13
6	4 : 5 : 10 : 11
7	10 : 14 : 15
8	12 : 16 : 17 : 18
9	9 : 17 : 19 : 20 : 9 : 10 : 11
10	14 : 15 : 10 : 11
11	4 : 21
12	17 : 13 : 3 : 22 : 9 : 11
13	14 : 15 : 10 : 11
14	13 : 23
15	6 : 7 : 8 : 9 : 9 : 10 : 11
16	14 : 15 : 10 : 11
17	4 : 21
18	17 : 13 : 3 : 22 : 9 : 11
19	24 : 25
20	1 : 13 : 19 : 10 : 11
21	26 : 27 : 28 : 4
22	8 : 12 : 28 : 10 : 11
23	8 : 14 : 15
24	Obliterated : 17 : 18 : 10 : 11
25	29 : 30 : 9
26	10 : 26 : 31 : 9
27	23 : 27 : 32 : 10 : 11
28	33 : 34 : 34
29	26 : 31 : 34
30	10 : 27 : 35
31	17 : 4 : 5 : 10 : 11

TABLE No 3

Rear Face

Phrase No.	Symbol Numbers
32	26 : 31
33	22 : 13 : 33 : 34
34	26 : 13 : 8 : 18 : 11
35	26 : 17 : 25 : 36 : 37
36	29 : 26 : 38 : 34 : 39
37	35 : 17 : 13 : 26
38	26 : 31 : 26
39	8 : 17 : 26
40	22 : 13 : 33 : 9
41	29 : 26 : 38 : 34 : 39
42	26 : 31 : 34
43	5 : 29 : 34
44	29 : 26 : 38 : 34
45	4 : 9 : 37 : 11
46	23 : 25 : 19 : 8 : 18
47	4 : 23 : 34
48	17 : 20 : 40
49	8 : 41 : 35 : 35 : 34
50	4 : 1 : 22 : 9
51	27 : 38 : 14 : 11
52	8 : 27 : 35 : 26
53	22 : 42 : 7 : 39
54	17 : 4 : 5 : 26 : 43
55	23 : 25 : 4 : 5
56	44 : 17 : 13 : 40
57	10 : 41 : 35 : 23
58	9 : 22 : 39
59	45 : 13 : 7 : 11
60	8 : 26 : 31 : 9
61	26 : 27 : 39 : 10 : 11

5. The Forty-five Symbols

Eight-Petalled Rosette

This simple design is found on many artifacts which have been unearthed throughout the Mediterranean area. Sometimes referred to as a Sun symbol, it is used as a decorative device to show the regard that is held for the recipient of the item.

Also found in the ruins of the Earlier palace at Phaistos was a distinctive pedestal bowl in Kamares ware with sculptured eight-petalled rosettes as a three-dimensional ornament.

From other parts of Minoan Crete, the Cup of Eggshell ware from the Earlier palace at Knossos (Fig. 2) and the minature seal found in the early circular tomb at Agia Triada (Fig. 3) also display this particular design.

This association of the Sun with persons considered to be of high rank or status is therefore an attempt to convey in an artistic way the concept of royalty.

Thus, as used on the Disk it can be assigned the word **ROYAL**.

Fig. 2

Fig. 3

A female figurine with a rosette painted upon her cheeks was unearthed at Mycenae.

Shaven-Headed Man

This symbol is the profile of the central character of the Disk. It only appears in this form in the opening phrases, and thereafter is represented by Symbols Nos. 4,32 and 45. My interpretation of these phrases leads me to the conclusion that this profile is possibly a death mask of the central character. The figure-of-eight cheek markings were probably applied after death and are a Minoan funereal rite.

An impression from a Minoan portrait seal found in the Palace of Knossos* (Fig. 4) shows a similarity in the physiognomy of these two heads which cannot be denied.

In keeping with the activities of the central character of the Disk, I have dubbed him the **"PEACEMAKER"**.

Fig. 4

Some scholars consider that shaved heads denote youth.

* Palace of Minos I   Fig. 201   Arthur Evans   1921-35

SYMBOL No. 3

Arrow

Though not a warlike people, the Minoans nevertheless used the bow and arrow for hunting purposes.*

Such was the skill of the maker of the Disk in carving fine details, that one must consider that the omission of the arrowhead i.e. only the shaft and feathers are shown, was an intentional act.

Could it be that the maker of the Disk was trying to convey an arrow embedded in the body of the victim?

This symbol is therefore an ideogram, used on the Disk to convey the concept of **DEATH**.

The Minoan kilt appears to have been worn by young persons of high social standing.

SYMBOL No. 4

Striding Man

This symbol shows the central character of the Disk - the "Peacemaker" on his travels. He is shown barefooted, naked to the waist and wearing a short skirt or kilt. This particular mode of dress is illustrated on certain Minoan frescoes and gems.

Though not the regular costume of the palace age, it survived in mythological and ceremonial scenes.

The determined gait of the figure conveys the resolution of purpose with which the central character pursues his objective.

Thus this symbol conveys **STRIDING ON**.

* Crete and Early Greece.   Pg. 157   F. Matz   1962

32

Ear of Corn

The cultivation of wheat and barley enabled the Hunter-gatherers to cease their nomadic wanderings and settle on the land; thus establishing the first communities.

Here on the Disk, the **EAR OF CORN** is carried by the "Peace-maker" as a symbol of peace and goodwill.

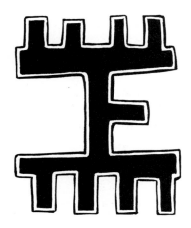

Place Glyph

An example of the Egyptian influence that pervades the Disk is this hieroglyphic place glyph. These signs, denoting a village or a Camp often show recognizable characteristics or similarities to the actual place.

On the slate palette of King Narmer from Hierakonpolis, a further example of a place glyph is shown (See Fig. 5)

As used on the Disk, the symbol appears to be the plan view of a **CAMP** with nine seperate living spaces.

Palette of Narmer
(Detail)

Fig. 5

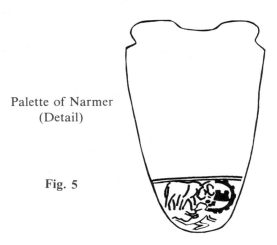

SYMBOL No. 7

Stalk of Flax

Second only in importance to Corn, the cultivation of **FLAX** from which cotton could be obtained contributed to a more settled life style by enabling rough clothing to be made.

SYMBOL No. 8

Flower Blossom

The use of decorative plant motives, including tulips and lilies adapted from the backgrounds of contemporary palace frescoes as patterns for pottery of the early stages of the second palaces (MM III, 1700-1550 B.C.) are synonomous with the naturalism of Minoan art.*

This symbol on the Disk appears to be another symbol of peace and goodwill carried by the "Peacemaker".

* Minoan and Mycenaean Art   Pg. 29   Reynold Higgins   1967

SYMBOL No.9

Animal's Hide

This symbol is used throughout the Disk both as evidence of the slaughter of animals by the Hunters and incorporated in the Place Name as a sign of affluence.

The **ANIMAL'S HIDE** as it appears in the Place Name (Phrases 3 and 15) is used in a unique manner. The neck of the animal pointing downwards when the occupants of the Camp are in residence, and upwards when they are away from the site.

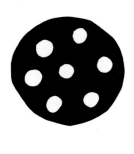

SYMBOL No. 10

Seven Dots (Encircled)

The first form of writing used in Minoan Crete was a hieroglyphic script derived from Egyptian models.*

The simple numbering system which in Egypt consisted of the numbers 1 to 9 being represented by the appropriate number of dashes was followed closely by the Minoan Linear A and B systems.

On the Phaistos Disk, dots are used to indicate the numbers one to nine; thus this particular symbol on the Disk indicates the number **SEVEN.**

This simple use of dots to indicate numbers also occurs on the last phrase dividers at the end of both the front and rear faces. The implications of this are discussed further on Pg. 116

* Minoan and Mycenaean Art   Pg. 18   Reynold Higgins   1967

SYMBOL No. 11

Man with Headdress

One must look beyond the shores of Minoan Crete to find the origins of the people who possessed these distinctive profiles.

According to the studies of Flinders Petrie, amongst the seperate types of people inhabiting Ancient Egypt in the Pre-dynastic and Proto-dynastic periods were "an aquiline type representative of a white-skinned Libyan race".*

Libyan captives as depicted on Egyptian temple basreliefs are recognizable by the feathers they wore as a headdress.**

The coastal strip of Libya lies only some 300 kms. (190 mls) from the southern coast of Crete.

As shown on the Disk, this symbol represents the **HUNTERS.**
When preceded by Symbol No. 10 refers to SEVEN HUNTERS.
When not preceded by symbol No. 10 refers to a LONE HUNTER.

  * Central History of Africa II   Pg. 30   UNESCO
 ** Central History of Africa II   Pg. 139   UNESCO

SYMBOL No. 12

Implement

An implement for making a furrow in the ground in which a seed of corn could be planted was one of the first simple agricultural tools to be used by early man.

In order to instruct others in the cultivation of crops and as a sign of goodwill, the **HAND PLOUGH** was a tool of immense value.

See also Symbol No. 32 (Man carrying Object)

SYMBOL No. 13

Torch

This symbol appears to be a combined pictogram and ideogram, for it represents both literally a **TORCH** and the idea of **NIGHT-TIME.** As shown on the Disk, it consists of a carrying handle and an enlarged cage for holding the burning flax.

Flying Bird   **Speech Curl**

In the eastern corner of the Throne Room of the Mycenaean Palace of Nestor at Pylos (Ano Englianos) in the Western Peloponnese were found fragments of a scene showing a male figure seated on a rock playing a lyre.* A Flying Bird with wings outstretched is shown moving away from the instrument. (Fig. 6) Was this an attempt to depict melodious music wafting from the strings? The people of the Greek mainland adopted the art of wall-painting from Crete and the first paintings there may have been the work of Cretan artists.*

Could the Flying Bird on the Disk from Phaistos also represent sound travelling from one place (or person) to another? In Phrases 13 and 16 the Flying Bird with Symbol No. 14 is shown travelling towards the Hunter (Symbol No. 11) In Phrase No. 10 it is shown travelling away from the Hunters; and in Phrases 7 and 23 travelling upwards (to the skies?)

Was this symbol of the Flying Bird meant to convey that words or a message passed between the "Peacemaker" and the Hunters? Thus, by the simple device of altering the orientation of the Flying Bird the maker of the Disk was able to convey either **"A MESSAGE TO ......"** or **"A MESSAGE FROM ......"** or a **"MESSAGE TO THE SKIES"**.

What of the companion symbol to the Flying Bird with which it is paired on each of the five occasions that it is shown on the Disk. Is this a form of Speech Curl? (A hieroglyphic sign used to depict words or sounds issuing from the mouth) ...... Could it indicate a shout? Did the "Peacemaker" shout to attract the attention of his quarry, the no-madic Hunters? Did they in turn shout a warning or greeting?

Its association with the message sign indicates that the warning or greeting was **SHOUTED.**

Fig. 6

One is reminded of Homer's beautiful phrase 'winged words'.

This fresco reconstructed in water colour by Piet de Jong can be seen in the **Museum at Chora in the Peloponnese.**

* Guide to the Palace of Nestor.   Pg. 11   Univ. of Cincinnati   1967
* The Arts in Prehistoric Greece.   Pg. 77   Sinclair Hood   1978

Piece of Pottery

Another of the gifts carried by the "Peacemaker" on his journey is this **SHALLOW DISH** complete with seperate lid and shaped centre handle.

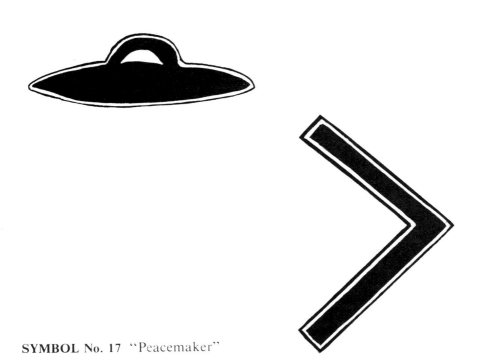

SYMBOL No. 17 "Peacemaker"

Direction Sign

From time immemorial this symbol has been used to indicate direction or movement between two locations. In (Sir) Arthur Evans authorative work on Minoan Crete; Palace of Minos Vol. I in which he published many of the Cretan hieroglyphs or conventionalized pictograms, which he had found inscribed on various clay tablets and sealings, this particular symbol is included. (Fig. 214 No. 42)

Throughout the Disk this symbol is used to indicate the fact that the central character was **TRAVELLING ON.**

SYMBOL No. 18

Actual Size

Seated Female

This exquisitely detailed pictogram represents the female companions of the Hunters.

It is interesting to note that even though the body is shown from the front the head and feet are shown in profile.

She is shown seated with a small child lying face down across her lap.

She has long straight hair. Her breasts are uncovered and she wears an ankle-length skirt. This particular style of dress is distinctly Minoan.

A well known example of this fashion is the Snake-Goddess from Knossos. (Fig. 7). This statuette can be seen in Case 50 Room IV Heraklion Museum.

As shown on the Disk this symbol represents the **WOMEN.**

Fig. 7

SYMBOL No. 19

Resting Bird

Just as the Flying Bird (Symbol No. 15) is used on the Disk to convey the idea of a message passing from one person to another, so this symbol is used to convey a **MESSAGE RECEIVED.**

SYMBOL No. 20

Rock Formation

This pictogram represents a Megalithic landmark seen by the "Peacemaker" on his travels in North Africa. Shown on the Disk in only two dimensions, this rock formation was used as a **PLATFORM for the LIVING** and consisted of a large slab of rock serving as a roof, supported on two smaller rocks.

Rock Column

This is a pictogram representing a natural landmark. These rock columns are formed by vertical erosion, where the hard rock on top has prevented the erosion of the soil directly underneath it.

Examples of this phenomenon can be found today in the Sahara desert.*

* The Desert   A. Starker Leopold   1963

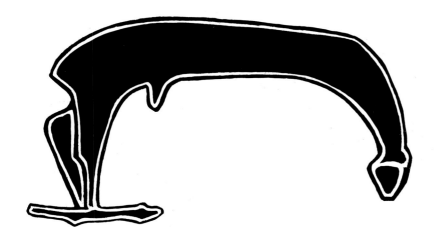

Grazing Animal

In order to conserve linear space this symbol has been printed on the Disk sideways i.e. it has been turned through 90°. Five other symbols have been treated the same way. They are symbols Nos. 16, 20, 23, 31 and 42.

It is shown here viewed from the normal direction of progress when reading the Disk. That is from left to right; from the centre to the rim.

In my opinion this is a picture of an animal grazing. Its long, slim neck is turned towards the observer, thus hiding the front legs. The animal is obviously male and is shown standing on marshy ground.

In (Sir) Arthur Evans magnificent work. "Palace of Minos" in which he considers the Disk, a complete Table of Symbols is shown. Unfortunately, this symbol, as well as three other symbols are depicted upside down! In consequence of this error, many other researchers who have not examined the actual Disk have identified this particular symbol as a ship. Whilst a cursory glance may show a certain similarity, the lack of either masts, rigging, sails or oars-features consistently shown on representations of Minoan (Cretan) ships-highlights the error.

On the Disk this symbol represents **HERDS OF GRAZING ANIMALS.**

Note: - This criticism applies to Symbols Nos. 20, 21 and 44.

SYMBOL No. 23

Fish

This symbol is an ideogram used throughout the Disk to represent the **SEA.**

Though not identical, the configuration of fins and tail bears a close similarity to the decoration on the Beak-spouted Jug. Kamares Ware from Vassiliki. East Crete. Middle Minoan I and now on display in the Heraklion Museum.

SYMBOL No. 24

Bow

Careful examination of this symbol reveals that the bowstring has been neatly tied to the body of the bow, thus rendering it unusable.

In this way it probably indicates the cessation of hunting or even armed conflict.

Thus this is an ideogram used to convey the concept of **PEACE.**

SYMBOL No. 25

Empty Husk

Representing the end of a period of time, this ideogram occurs four times on the Disk. The empty husk that is left when the ripe corn has been harvested is used to depict the **END OF HARVEST TIME.**

It can be deduced from this that the legend of the Phaistos Disk covers at least four years.

SYMBOL No. 26

Water Container

Paired with Symbol No. 31 (Water Sign) on six occasions throughout the Disk, this symbol is a combined ideogram and pictogram. Firstly, it represents literally a container for carrying water-probably a sheep's stomach and secondly it is used to indicate the length of journey undertaken i.e. the distance that could be travelled before the contents are expended.

The **WATER CONTAINER** occurs repeatedly in the second half of the legend, thus signifying the change of conditions.

SYMBOL No. 27

Libation Vase

Containing wine or various fruits, the **LIBATION VASE** was left besides shrines as a gift to the gods. They have been discovered in graves presumably buried with the dead. At a site at Sphougaras on Crete they had apparently been placed in the earth upside down*, as shown on the Disk.

* Mycenae and the Mycenaean Age   Mylonas   1966

SYMBOL No. 28

In the treasury at Triadha, some nineteen ox-hide shaped bronze ingots, each weighing approx. 29.5 kg were found.

Shaped Object

This curiously shaped object which appears only twice on the Disk, is possibly an **INGOT** of copper or other precious metal.

Large ingots of copper shaped like an ox's hide and carried on the shoulders of Cretans are shown on the tomb paintings at the Tomb of Rekhmire (c. 1470 B.C.) in Egypt. (Fig. 8) They were amongst the many gifts or tributes which the Minoans brought to the Egyptians, with whom they had strong trade relations.

Man of Keftiu
Tomb of Rekhmire, Thebes
After Davies.

Fig. 8

Hand-Shaped Mark

Early man made coloured hand-prints or outlined his hand in colour, normally with red ochre or black.*

It was the practice amongst nomadic people to place their hand upon a rock face and scribe around it. By leaving their mark in this way they were indicating, "We were at this place" to all who came after. This symbol first appears on the Disk in Phrase 25 and would therefore have assisted the "Peacemaker" to follow the trail of the Hunters.

A cave drawing from Tassili in the Sahara bears some similarity to this symbol on the Disk with lines drawn around the wrist in a similar way. (Fig. 9)

Fig. 9

* Prehistoric and Ancient Art   Pg. 16   René Huyghe   1981

SYMBOL No. 30

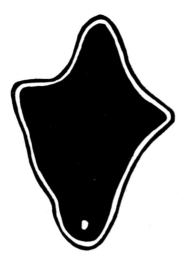

Animal's Skin

This symbol represents another **ANIMAL'S SKIN** found by the "Peacemaker" as he follows the trail of the Hunters. It is this continual finding of the evidence of this wanton killing amongst the herds of livestock that motivates the "Peacemaker".

SYMBOL No. 31

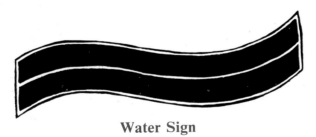

Water Sign

Many different cultures throughout the world have used this particular symbol or close variations of it to represent water. The Egyptian hieroglyphic sign for water (Fig. 10) clearly demonstrates how these Minoan signs owe much to their neighbours.

On the Disk this symbol is always shown together with the Water Container and thus represents a fresh water **RIVER**.

　　　　Fig. 10

Man carrying Object

Here we see the "Peacemaker" carrying a Hand-plough (See Symbol No. 12) beneath his right arm.

The dotted line is a damaged part of the print.

SYMBOL No. 33

Resting Animal

This is a pictogram representing an animal viewed from behind.

Shown on the Disk paired with the Torch (Symbol No. 13) which indicates Night-time, the animal is thus shown resting at night.

Thus this symbol depicts **HERDS OF RESTING ANIMALS.**

Animal's Head

The existence of hounds used as Hunting dogs by the Minoans is attested by various seals and frescoes found in Crete and elsewhere in the Minoan sphere of artistic influence.*

On the Phaistos Disk the symbol of the hound's head is used in three different ways. Firstly, it is shown in Phrase 28 twice in echelon-indicating a pack of hunting dogs.

Secondly, it is shown singly representing its role as a companion to its master. In the third variation, the **HOUND** is depicted with its snout pointing up in the air, as if lying on its back. This probably indicates that the hound is dead, and has been killed by its master in order to provide food for both himself and his remaining hounds, when no other source of food is available.

---

* Impressions and seals from both Agia Triadha and Knossos. Also a remarkable hound's head in stone from Knossos.

SYMBOL No. 35

Large Structure

The man-made structure shown in this symbol stands some 8 metres in height, as scaled from the front entrance. Its ornate architecture with a balcony and ornamental shaped supports would have required many hours of labour to construct it.

This cupola shape was apparently well known to the potters in Lower Egypt in the Pre-dynastic period,* whilst some tenuous evidence exists for the building of pillared structures on Crete which seem to represent circular shrines.**

On the Disk it appears to be a **TEMPLE** or similar place of worship.

SYMBOL No. 36

Animal's Skull

This symbol of an **ANIMAL'S SKULL** is used to convey the waterless terrain through which the "Peacemaker" travels on his journey.

* Egyptian Art   Pg. 134   De Rachewiltz   1960
** The Arts in Prehistoric Greece   Pg. 23   Sinclair Hood   1978

Small Structure

This symbol represents a one-man **TENT.** In the earliest times North Africa was the home of nomadic hunters who probably dwelt in light and easily portable tents, to protect themselves in particular from the heat, since in those days the climate was semi-tropical.*

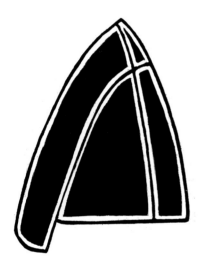

SYMBOL No. 38

Dried-up Plant

This is an ideogram used to convey the lack of drinking water. It is shown adjacent to the Water Container (Symbol. 26) when this is in an **EMPTY** condition.

The shrivelled appearance of the leaves and the soil-free roots convey the dryness of the terrain.

It is interesting to note that this symbol also appears on one occasion adjacent to the Libation Vase (Symbol No. 27)

* Egyptian Art   Pg. 132   De Rachewiltz   1960

SYMBOL No. 39

Torso with Legs

This symbol is an ideogram used to convey the sense of being **LOST.**

Lacking both a head and a pair of feet, it thus indicates losing one's bearings and being unable to proceed.

SYMBOL No. 40

Animal's Skin

Used in an identical manner to Symbol No. 30, this symbol of another **ANIMAL'S SKIN** is further evidence of the killing of the Hunters.

SYMBOL No. 41

Shaped Container

This symbol represents another container. It is used to carry gifts, possibly of fruit or wine and these are left outside the temple in gratitude presumably to the Gods-for favours granted or the safe return from a long or hazardous journey.

The striped effect is reminiscent of the stone vases from Mochlos.

On each of the two occasions that this **WINE JUG** symbol appears on the Disk it is next to the symbol for the Temple. (Symbol No. 35)

SYMBOL No. 42

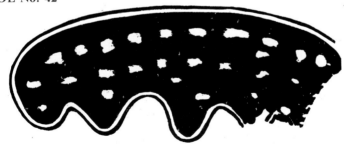

Crocodile

This symbol is a pictorial representation of a **CROCODILE** thrashing about in a turbulent river. An unforgettable sight to the traveller on the river bank.

Axe-Adze

Another tool of great importance to early man. Used in forest clearance and in the preparation of ground for eventual cultivation, the **AXE-ADZE** has been found at many ancient sites throughout the world.

At Chamaizi, Crete similarly shaped implements were found.* These are usually in the form of the blade only, the wooden haft having perished over the years.

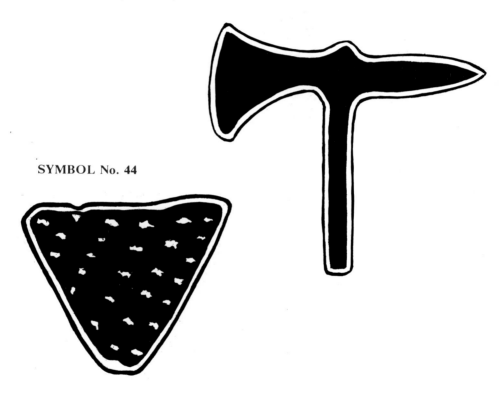

SYMBOL No. 44

Basket

The pattern of markings duplicates the effect of interwoven reeds. Used as a container for fruit or vegetables, this symbol is a pictogram of a **BASKET.**

* Handbuch der Vorgeschichte   1974

Stationary Man

This symbol is a pictorial representation of the Central Character - the "Peacemaker" standing forlorn and dejected. He is lost. He has no more drinking water and most of his edible hounds have been eaten. He has also failed to find his quarry.

So the **"PEACEMAKER" STOOD** considering no doubt his predicament.

6. Tables of Frequency

TABLE No. 4

Symbols -- Frequency of Occurence

Symbol No.		Freq.	Symbol No.		Freq.
11	Man with Headdress	19	25	Empty Husk	4
26	Water Container	18	38	Dried-up Plant	4
10	Seven Dots (Encl)	17	12	Implement	3
9	Animal's Hide	15	19	Resting Bird	3
17	Direction Sign	12	33	Resting Animal	3
4	Striding Man	11	2	Shaven-Hd. Man	2
8	Flower Blossom	11	6	Place Glyph	2
13	Torch	11	20	Rock Formation	2
34	Animal's Head	11	21	Rock Column	2
22	Grazing Animal	7	28	Ingot	2
5	Ear of Corn	6	37	Small Structure	2
14	Speech Curl	6	40	Animal's Skin	2
23	Fish	6	41	Shaped Container	2
27	Libation Vase	6	16	Piece of Pottery	1
31	Water Sign	6	24	Bow	1
35	Large Structure	6	30	Animal's Skin	1
15	Flying Bird	5	32	Man carrying Object	1
29	Hand-shaped Mark	5	36	Animal's Skull	1
39	Torso with Legs	5	42	Crocodile	1
1	Eight-petalled Ros.	4	43	Axe-Adze	1
3	Embedded Arrow	4	44	Basket	1
7	Stalk of Flax	4	45	Stationary Man	1
18	Seated Female	4			

TABLE No. 5

Pairs of Symbols

Symbol Nos.   **Frequency**

10 : 11	Seven Dots (Encl)	Man with Headdress	13
4 : 5	Striding Man	Ear of Corn	5
14 : 15	Speech Curl	Flying Bird	5
26 : 31	Water Container	Water Sign	5
17 : 13	Direction Sign	Torch	3
8 : 12	Flower Blossom	Implement	2
8 : 18	Flower Blossom	Seated Female	2
4 : 21	Striding Man	Rock Column	2
17 : 18	Direction Sign	Seated Female	2
23 : 25	Fish	Empty Husk	2
26 : 27	Water Container	Libation Vase	2
22 : 9	Grazing Animal	Animal's Hide	2
27 : 35	Libation Vase	Large Structure	2
33 : 34	Resting Animal	Animal's Head	2
41 : 35	Shaped Container ...	Large Structure	2

Triple Symbols

1 : 2 : 3	Eight-ptld Ros ..... Shvn-Hd. Man..... Arrow	2
22 : 13 : 33	Grazing Animal ... Torch....Resting Animal	2
17 : 4 : 5	Direction Sign ...... Striding man...Ear of Corn	2
26 : 31 : 9	Water Container .. Water Sign .... Animal's Hide	2
26 : 31 : 34	Water Container .. Water Sign ... Animal's Head	2

Four Symbols

14 : 15 : 10 : 11	Speech Curl .. Flying Bird .. Seven Dots. Man with Headdress	3
29 : 26 : 38 : 34	Hand-shpd. Mrk .. Wtr.Cont .. Drd-up Plnt .. Animal's Head	3

TABLE No. 6

Like pairs

Nos.

9 : 9	Many Hides
26 : 26	Many Water Containers
34 : 34	Many Hounds
35 : 35	Many Temples

TABLE No. 7

Humans	2, 4, 11, 18, 32 and 45.
Animals, Birds, Fishes, Skins.	9, 15, 19, 22, 23, 30, 33, 34, 36, 40 and 42.
Flowers, Plants.	1, 5, 7, 8, 25 and 38.
Tools, Weapons.	3, 12, 13, 16, 24 and 43.
Containers.	26, 27, 41 and 44.
Structures.	35 and 37
Landmarks.	20 and 21.
Others.	6, 10, 14, 17, 28, 29, 31 and 39.

7. The Sixty-one Phrases

INTRODUCTION

Phrases 1 - 3

In these first three phrases the maker of the Disk informs us as to the identity of the Central Character and of his intentions. The name of his quarry and their possible whereabouts and the resolution with which he sets out to contact them is also depicted.

Note: The Key Words from each of the individual symbols have been linked to make intelligible phrases.

Front Face

(This is the story of the)

ROYAL "PEACEMAKER"   **DEATH**

(who has met his)

PHRASE No. 1 _____

(He went)

STRIDING ON   **EAR OF CORN**

(with a peace-token of an)

PHRASE No. 2 _____

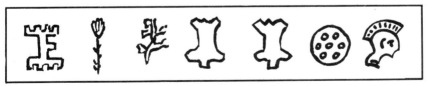

(to find the)

**CAMP   FLAX   FLOWER   BLOSSOM   MANY HIDES
SEVEN   HUNTERS**

(amidst)   (and)   (of the)

PHRASE No. 3 _____

First Journey

Phrases 4-7

In addition to the sample of corn, he takes some flower blossoms, a hand-plough and a torch - calling out many times to announce his approach.

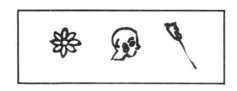

(The)

ROYAL **"PEACEMAKER"** **DEATH**

(who has met his)

PHRASE No. 4

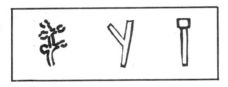

(took with him some)

FLOWER **BLOSSOM** **HAND PLOUGH** **TORCH**

(a) (and a)

PHRASE No. 5

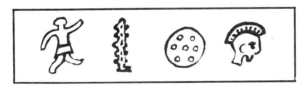

(and continued) (to find the)

STRIDING ON **EAR OF CORN** **SEVEN HUNTERS**

(with the peace token of the)

PHRASE No. 6

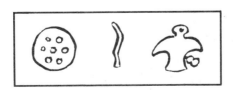

SEVEN (times he) **SHOUTED** (a) **MESSAGE TO THE SKIES**

PHRASE No. 7

Phrases 8 - 11

With the hand-plough and a shallow dish, he then visited a woman - possibly the wife of one of the hunters.

It appears that he now had information that his quarry; the group of seven hunters could be found at a particular landmark. Encouraged by the calls of the hunters, he carried on past the rock column landmark.

(then taking the) **HAND PLOUGH** (and a) **SHALLOW DISH** (he) **TRAVELLED ON** (towards the) **WOMEN**

PHRASE No. 8

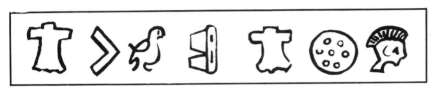

(Finding an) **ANIMAL'S HIDE** (he) **TRAVELLED ON.** (For he had) **RECEIVED A MESSAGE** (that, at the) **PLATFORM FOR THE LIVING** (he would find another) **ANIMAL'S HIDE** (and the) **SEVEN HUNTERS.**

PHRASE No. 9

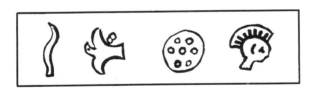

(He heard a) **SHOUTED MESSAGE FROM** (the) **SEVEN HUNTERS**

PHRASE No. 10

(but continued) **STRIDING ON** (towards the) **ROCK COLUMN** (landmark)

PHRASE No. 11

Phrases 12 - 15

Finding further evidence of the wanton killing of livestock, he again tried to attract the attention of the hunters by shouting to them. Reaching the sea, he found the hunter's camp — but they were not there.

TRAVELLING ON (through the) **NIGHT TIME** (he found) **DEATH** (amongst the) **HERDS OF GRAZING ANIMALS** (and another) **ANIMAL'S HIDE** (left by a) **HUNTER**

PHRASE No. 12

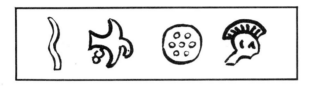

(He) **SHOUTED** (another) **MESSAGE** (to the) **SEVEN HUNTERS**

PHRASE No. 13

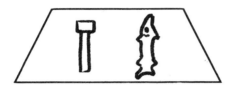

(That) **NIGHT TIME** (he reached the) **SEA**

PHRASE No. 14

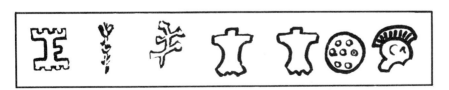

(and found the) **CAMP** (amidst) **FLAX, FLOWER BLOSSOM** (and) **MANY HIDES** (of the) **SEVEN HUNTERS.**

PHRASE No. 15

Phrases 16 - 19

Again he called out to the hunters before retracing his steps-passing the rock column landmark once more.

He returned through the pastures where he had found the dead animals.

At last came peace. It was the end of harvest time.

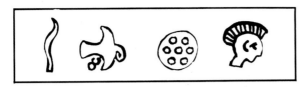

(Again he) **SHOUTED** (a) **MESSAGE** (to the) **SEVEN HUNTERS**

PHRASE No. 16
_____

(and once more he went) **STRIDING ON** (past the) **ROCK COLUMN** (land-mark)

PHRASE No. 17
_____

TRAVELLING ON (through the) **NIGHT TIME** (he again found) **DEATH** (amongst the) **HERDS OF GRAZING ANIMALS** (and another) **ANIMAL'S HIDE** (left by a) **LONE HUNTER.**

PHRASE No. 18
_____

(But now came) **PEACE.** (It was the) **END OF HARVEST TIME.**

PHRASE No. 19
_____

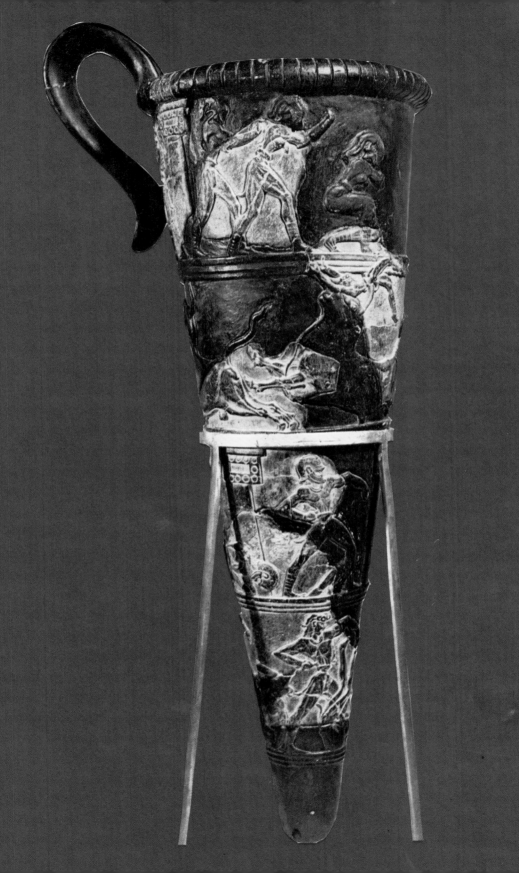

Second Journey

Phrases 20 - 23

The message received during the night encouraged the "Peacemaker" to embark on another journey. This time he takes a water container, libation vases and ingots of precious metal, in addition to the hand-plough and the corn samples.

Did his message to the skies refer to the fact that he was coming in peace, and was bringing flowers with him as a token of his goodwill?

(Then this) **ROYAL** (person; during the) **NIGHT TIME   RECEIVED A MESSAGE** (from the) **SEVEN HUNTERS.**

PHRASE No. 20

(Carrying a) **WATER CONTAINER** (a) **LIBATION VASE** (and an) **INGOT** (he went) **STRIDING ON**

PHRASE No. 21

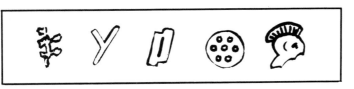

(With) **FLOWER BLOSSOM** (the) **HAND PLOUGH** (and the) **INGOT** (for the) **SEVEN HUNTERS.**

PHRASE No. 22

(Carrying the) **FLOWER BLOSSOM** (he) **SHOUTED** (a) **MESSAGE TO THE SKIES.**

PHRASE No. 23

Phrases 24 - 27

He visits the wives of the seven hunters and discovers the curious hand-shaped mark, skins and more hides.

Did the "Peacemaker" fill several water containers because he knew that he was approaching a desert?

He reaches the coast, leaving a libation vase as a sign of gratitude and, with the hand-plough tucked under his arm, heads for the seven hunters.

(With the) **OBLITERATED** (he) **TRAVELLED ON** (to the) **WOMEN** (of the) **SEVEN HUNTERS.**

PHRASE No. 24

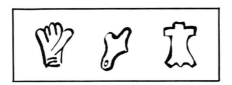

(He now found a) **HAND-SHAPED MARK** (and a) **ANIMAL'S SKIN** (and a) **ANIMAL'S HIDE.**

PHRASE No. 25

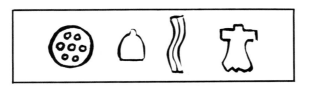

(He filled) **SEVEN WATER CONTAINERS** (at the) **RIVER** (and found another) **ANIMAL'S HIDE.**

PHRASE No. 26

(At the) **SEA** (coast he left a) **LIBATION VASE** (and) **CARRIED THE HAND PLOUGH** (to give to the) **SEVEN HUNTERS.**

PHRASE No. 27

Phrases 28 - 31

Travelling on with his pack of hounds, the need for fresh water becomes vital. He is forced to kill one of his hounds to provide food.

He leaves seven (several) libation vases at a circular shrine before moving on as resolutely as ever.

(Passing) **HERDS OF RESTING ANIMALS** (he journeyed on with his) **MANY HOUNDS.**

PHRASE No. 28

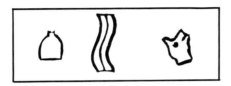

(Filling his) **WATER CONTAINER** (at the) **RIVER** (he killed a) **HOUND FOR FOOD.**

PHRASE No. 29

(He now left) **SEVEN LIBATION VASES** (at the) **TEMPLE.**

PHRASE No. 30

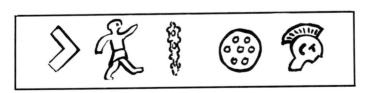

TRAVELLING ON (he went) **STRIDING ON** (with a peace token of an) **EAR OF CORN** (towards the) **SEVEN HUNTERS.**

PHRASE No. 31

Phrases 32 - 35

The vital necessity for finding fresh water is emphasised. The lack of food again forces him to kill one of his hounds.

Does he present the flower blossoms to the wife of the lone hunter?

It is the end of the second harvest (year) since his journeys began.

Such are the waterless conditions of the terrain through which he is now passing, that he discovers the whitened skulls of dead animals.

Rear Face

(He filled another) **WATER CONTAINER** (at the) **RIVER**

PHRASE No. 32

(He walked on past) **HERDS OF GRAZING ANIMALS** (and on through the) **NIGHT TIME** (passing) **HERDS OF RESTING ANIMALS** (before he killed another) **HOUND FOR FOOD.**

PHRASE No. 33

(After travelling for another) **WATER CONTAINERS** (length of journey through the) **NIGHT TIME** (with) **FLOWER BLOSSOM** (for the) **WOMAN** (of the) **LONE HUNTER:**

PHRASE No. 34

(With only one) **WATER CONTAINER** (he) **TRAVELLED ON.** (It was the) **END OF** (the second) **HARVEST TIME.** (He came across an) **ANIMAL'S SKULL** (and an empty) **TENT.**

PHRASE No. 35

Phrases 36 - 39

Following the trail of hand-shaped marks he journeys on across the desert. At times his water container is empty. He walks through the cool of the night to avoid the heat of the day. For many miles he travels, obtaining water wherever possible.

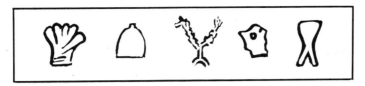

(Here he found another) **HAND-SHAPED MARK.** (But now his) **WATER CONTAINER** (was) **EMPTY.** (He killed another) **HOUND FOR FOOD** (but now he was) **LOST.**

PHRASE No. 36

(From the) **TEMPLE** (he went) **TRAVELLING ON** (through the) **NIGHT TIME** (for another) **WATER CONTAINERS** (length of journey)

PHRASE No. 37

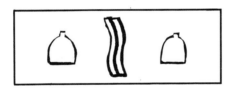

(Filling the) **WATER CONTAINER** (at the) **RIVER** (he crossed it and continued on for another) **WATER CONTAINERS** (length of journey)

PHRASE No. 38

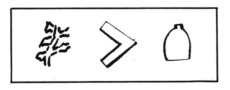

(With) **FLOWER BLOSSOM** (he) **TRAVELLED ON** (for another) **WATER CONTAINERS** (length of journey)

PHRASE No. 39

Phrases 40 - 43

Through numerous herds of cattle he walks on. Following the hand-shaped marks, his hounds running at his side, unsure of his directions and with little water.

He decides to leave a sample of corn and one of his hounds besides a hand-shaped marker.

(Passing) **HERDS OF GRAZING ANIMALS** (and on through the) **NIGHT TIME** (he passed behind) **HERDS OF RESTING ANIMALS** (where he came upon another) **AMINAL'S HIDE.**

PHRASE No. 40

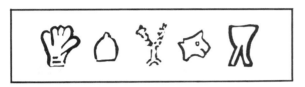

(Again he found a) **HAND-SHAPED MARK.** (But now his) **WATER CONTAINER** (was again) **EMPTY.** (He still had a) **HOUND AS A COMPANION** (But once again he was) **LOST.**

PHRASE No. 41

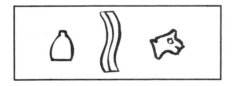

(Continuing onwards, he was eventually able to fill his) **WATER CONTAINER** (at a) **RIVER** (and continued onward with his) **HOUND AS A COMPANION.**

PHRASE No. 42

(He left an) **EAR OF CORN** (besides the) **HAND-SHAPED MARK** (and one of his) **HOUNDS.**

PHRASE No. 43

Phrases 44 - 47

His difficult journey continues. Then he finds the tent of the lone hunter and reaches the sea again. It is now the end of the third harvest. Was he given directions by the wife of the lone hunter? Resoloutely he carried on along the coast.

(Beyond the) **HAND-SHAPED MARK** (his) **WATER CONTAINER** (was again) **EMPTY** (He killed a) **HOUND FOR FOOD.**

PHRASE No. 44

(He went) **STRIDING ON** (until he discovered an) **ANIMAL'S HIDE** (outside the) **TENT** (of a) **LONE HUNTER.**

PHRASE No. 45

(He reached the) **SEA** (coast again. It was the) **END OF HARVEST TIME** (for the third year. Here he) **RECEIVED A MESSAGE** (and took some) **FLOWER BLOSSOM** (to the) **WOMAN.**

PHRASE No. 46.

STRIDING ON (along the) **SEA** (coast, he killed another) **HOUND FOR FOOD.**

PHRASES No. 47

Phrases 48 - 51

At last he arrives at the landmark at which he had been told that he might find the seven hunters. It is near a place of many temples where he leaves flower blossom and wine jugs.

Finding the hides of cattle which he considered to be his own, he takes an empty libation vase and calls to the lone hunter.

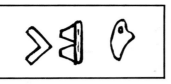

TRAVELLING ON (he came to a) **PLATFORM FOR THE LIVING** (where he found another) **ANIMAL'S SKIN.**

PHRASE No. 48

(He left) **FLOWER BLOSSOM** (and a) **WINE JUG** (besides the place of) **MANY TEMPLES** (and killed another) **HOUND FOR FOOD.**

PHRASE No. 49

(Now the Peacemaker was) **STRIDING ON** (through his own) **ROYAL HERDS OF GRAZING ANIMALS** (here he found another) **ANIMAL'S HIDE.**

PHRASE No. 50

(Carrying a) **LIBATION VASE** (though it was) **EMPTY** (he) **SHOUTED** (to the) **LONE HUNTER.**

PHRASE No. 51

Phrases 52 - 55

Leaving gifts for the gods at the temple he travels on. The sight of a crocodile thrashing about in the river is a memory not to be forgotten! Though lost, he walks on with an axe-adze in addition to the corn.

Reaching the coast sees the passing of the fourth harvest time since his journeys began. Yet he strides on as resolute as ever.

(Then leaving the) **FLOWER.BLOSSOM** (and the) **LIBATION VASE** (at the) **TEMPLE** (he took one) **WATER CONTAINER** (with him)

PHRASE No. 52

(Suddenly, after passing by) **HERDS OF GRAZING ANIMALS** (he was startled by the sight of a) **CROCODILE** (in the river flowing through fields of) **FLAX.** (But now he was again) **LOST.**

PHRASE No. 53

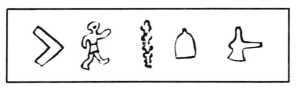

TRAVELLING ON (he went) **STRIDING ON** (with a peace token of an) **EAR OF CORN, WATER CONTAINER** (and a) **AXE-ADZE.**

PHRASE No. 54

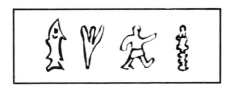

(Once again he came to the) **SEA** (coast. For the fourth year it was the) **END OF HARVEST TIME.** (yet still he went) **STRIDING ON** (with a peace token of an) **EAR OF CORN.**

PHRASE No. 55

Phrases 56 - 59

Ever onwards, often at night-the "Peacemaker" leaves several wine jugs at the shrine on the coast.

He still finds the occasional skins and hides of dead animals amongst the herds of cattle. Often he is uncertain as to his whereabouts and stands dejected during the long night searching for the hunter responsible for the killing.

(Carrying a) **BASKET** (he) **TRAVELLED ON** (through the) **NIGHT TIME** (and came across another) **ANIMAL'S SKIN.**

PHRASE No. 56
_____

(Then he left) **SEVEN WINE JUGS** (outside the) **TEMPLE** (on the) **SEA** (coast)

PHRASE No. 57
_____

(Again he found another) **ANIMAL'S HIDE** (amongst the) **HERDS OF GRAZING ANIMALS** (but once again he was) **LOST.**

PHRASE No. 58
_____

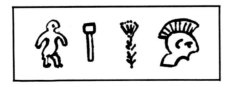

(So now the) **PEACEMAKER STOOD** (in the) **NIGHT TIME** (amongst the fields of) **FLAX** (of the) **LONE HUNTER.**

PHRASE No. 59
_____

Phrases 60 - 61

At the river that flows through the fields of flower blossoms he discovers another animal's hide which makes him renew his search.

But with only one water container and a libation vase he now realises that he has lost his quarry.

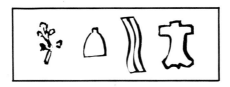

(By fields of) **FLOWER BLOSSOM** (he was able to fill a) **WATER CON-TAINER** (at the) **RIVER** (where he saw another) **ANIMAL'S HIDE.**

PHRASE No. 60

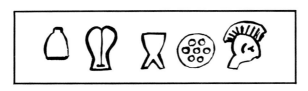

(With only one) **WATER CONTAINER** (and a) **LIBATION VASE** (he realised that he had) **LOST** (the) **SEVEN HUNTERS.**

PHRASE No. 61

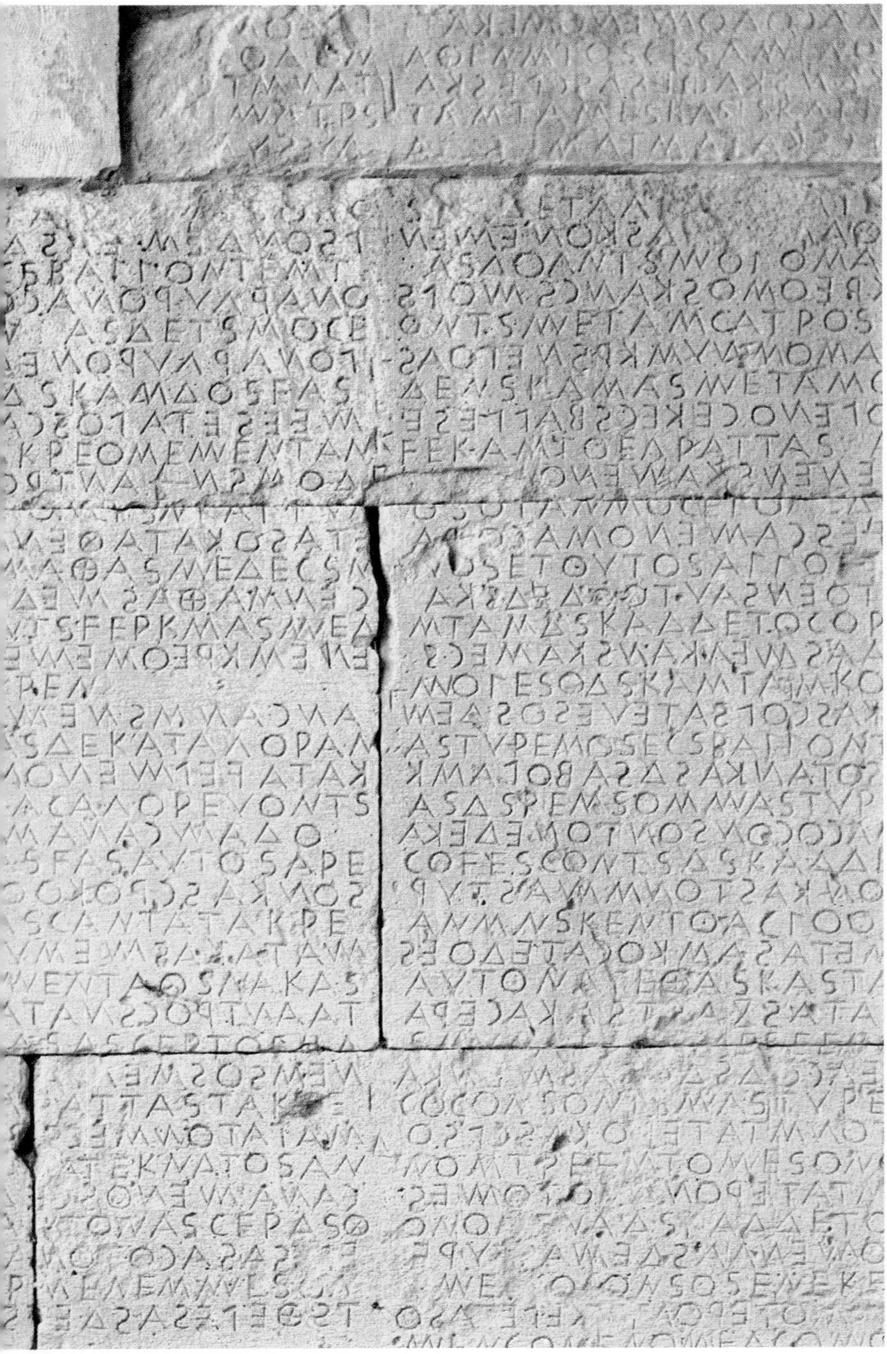

8. Legend of the Disk

Front Face

Phrase

1   This is the story of the Royal Peacemaker who has met his death.

2   He went striding on with a peace token of an ear of corn

3   to find the camp amidst flax, flower blossom and many hides of the seven hunters.

4   The Royal Peacemaker who has met his death

5   took with him some flower blossom a hand plough and a torch

6   and continued striding on with a peace token of an ear of corn to find the seven hunters.

7   Seven times he shouted a message to the skies

8   then taking the hand plough and a shallow dish he travelled on towards the women.

9   Finding an animal's hide he travelled on, for he had received a message that, at the platform for the living he would find another animal's hide and the seven hunters.

10   He heard a shouted message from the seven hunters

11   but continued striding on past the rock column landmark.

12   Travelling on through the night time he found death amongst the herds of grazing animals and another animal's hide left by a hunter.

13   He shouted another message to the seven hunters.

14   That night time he reached the sea.

15   and found the camp amidst flax, flower blossom and many hides of the seven hunters.

16   Again he shouted a message to the seven hunters

17   and once more he went striding on past the rock column land-
        mark.

18   Travelling on through the night time, he again found death
        amongst the herds of grazing animals and another animal's hide
        left by a lone hunter.

19   But now came peace. It was the end of harvest time.

20   Then this royal person; during the night time received a message
        from the seven hunters.

21   Carrying a water container, a libation vase and an ingot he went
        striding on

22   with flower blossom, the hand plough and the ingot for the seven
        hunters.

23   Carrying the flower blossom he shouted a message to the skies.

24   With the (Obliterated) he travelled on to the women of the seven
        hunters.

25   He now found a hand-shaped mark and an animal's skin and an
        animal's hide.

26   He filled seven water containers at the river and found another
        animal's hide.

27   At the sea-coast he left a libation vase and carried the hand-
        plough to give to the seven hunters.

28   Passing herds of resting animals he journeyed on with his many
        hounds.

29   Filling his water container at the river, he killed a hound for food.

30   He now left seven libation vases at the temple.

31   Travelling on, he went striding on with the peace token of an ear
        of corn towards the seven hunters.

Rear Face

32   He filled another water container at the river.

33   He walked on past herds of grazing animals and on through the night time passing herds of resting animals before he killed another hound for food.

34   After travelling for another water containers length of journey through the night time with flower blossom for the woman of the lone hunter.

35   With only one water container he travelled on. It was the end of the second harvest time. He came across an animal's skull and an empty tent.

36   Here he found another hand-shaped mark. But now his water container was empty. He killed another hound for food but now he was lost.

37   From the temple he went travelling on through the night time for another water containers length of journey.

38   Filling the water container at the river he crossed it and continued on for another water containers length of journey.

39   With flower blossom he travelled on for another water containers length of journey.

40   Passing herds of grazing animals and on through the night time. he passed behind herds of resting animals where he came upon another animal's hide.

41   Again he found a hand-shaped mark. But now his water container was again empty. He still had a hound as a companion, but once again he was lost.

42   Continuing onwards, he was eventually able to fill his water container at a river and continued onward with his hound as his companion.

43   He left an ear of corn besides the hand-shaped mark and one of his hounds.

44   Beyond the hand-shaped mark his water container was again empty. He killed a hound for food.

45   He went striding on until he discovered an animal's hide outside the tent of a lone hunter.

46   He reached the sea-coast again. It was the end of harvest time for the third year. Here he received a message and took some flower blossom to the woman.

47   Striding on along the sea-coast he killed another hound for food.

48   Travelling on he came to the platform for the living where he found another animal's skin.

49   He left flower blossom and a wine jug besides the place of many temples and killed another hound for food.

50   Now the Peacemaker was striding on through his own royal herds of grazing animals. Here he found another animal's hide.

51   Carrying a libation vase though it was empty, he shouted to the lone hunter.

52   Then, leaving the flower blossom and the libation vase at the temple, he took one water container with him.

53   Suddenly, after passing by herds of grazing animals he was startled by the sight of a crocodile in the river flowing through fields of flax. But now he was again lost.

54   Travelling on he went striding on with his peace token of the ear of corn, water container and a axe-adze.

55   Once again he came to the sea-coast. For the fourth year it was the end of harvest time; yet still he went striding on with the peace token of the ear of corn.

56   Carrying a basket he travelled on through the night time and came across another animal's skin.

57   Then he left seven wine jugs outside the temple on the sea-coast.

58   Again he found another animal's hide amongst the herds of grazing animals. But once again he was lost.

59   So now the Peacemaker stood in the night time amongst the fields of flax of the lone hunter.

60   By fields of flower blossom he was able to fill a water container at the river where he saw another animal's hide.

61   With only one water container and a libation vase he realised that he had lost the seven hunters.

9. Summary

Made almost 4000 years ago, the Disk from Phaistos is one of the earliest pictographic records to have been discovered anywhere throughout the world.

It is the printed record of the journeys of an early Minoan who crossed to the coast of North Africa and headed deeper into the harsh conditions of the Sahara in the hope of persuading one particular group of nomadic hunters to cease their destructive way of life.

As man began to cultivate primitive varieties of corn, so he was freed from the constant need to search for food. This in turn led to the establishment of settled community life as he ceased his nomadic wanderings. As the last remaining groups of hunter-gatherers passed through cultivated territory they caused considerable havoc, killing any livestock they could find to obtain meat and skins and stripping the land of fruit and crops.

This early Minoan set out on his mission of peace with samples of barley and flax, simple agricultural implements and other useful gifts.

The possibility that the Minoans crossed to the coast of North Africa was first suggested by (Sir) Arthur Evans.*

It has also been suggested that the style of chariots found in the Rock drawings at Fezzan and Tassili n'Ajjar is due to the influence of Cretan invaders who got lost in the Libyan desert sometime about 2000 B.C.** Such was the impact of the hazardous travels of this resolute Minoan, or the subsequent result of them, that an artist/craftsman decided to record for posterity the circumstances of these journeys.

Carving 45 tiny dies, each with a different symbol on its face and with the minuteness of details sharply defined, he impressed them onto a terra-cotta disk in a meaningful sequence.

Was the Disk carefully removed from its storage place on certain festive days and read to an attentive audience gathered around the courtyard of the Old Palace of Phaistos?

Examination of the last phrase divider at the end of both the front face and the rear face, shows that each of these faces was carefully numbered. The numbering system employed being the same as discussed on Page 36 in regard to Symbol No. 10, Seven Dots-Encircled. The Phaistos Disk as it is often referred to, being Sides 4 and 5 of what was originally a set of Disks. In its original form this set would have consisted of a protective Cover Disk; one can visualise the Eight-petalled Rosette (Symbol No 1) at its centre.

Sides 2 and 3 which have not yet been recovered. Sides 4 and 5 now on display in the Heraklion Museum, Crete and Sides 6 and 7 containing the unfinished part of the legend.

---

* Palace of Minos II   Pgs. 742-3   Arthur Evans   1921-35
** General History of Africa   Pg. 528   P. Salama   UNESCO

Following the destruction of the palace during a violent earthquake (c. 1700 B.C.) the Disk lay buried in the ruins for the next 3600 years before being unearthed by Doctor Pernier.

As stated earlier, certainly is not claimed and more material is required before proof can be ascertained. Nevertheless, the evidence presented here that more Disks may possibly still be buried beneath the earth in the Old Palace of Phaistos may inspire a further search by the current Italian team of archaeologists.

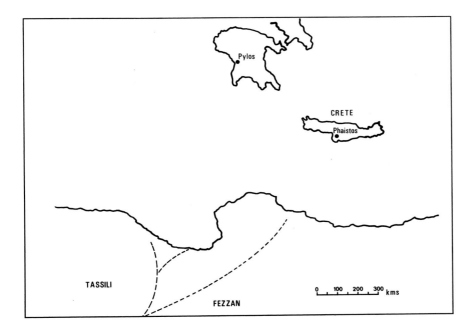

Fig. 11

Ancient Caravan routes across the Sahara (after M. Posnansky, 1971)

10. Bibliography

1	Cleator P.E.	Lost Languages	Hale and Co.	1959
2	Cottrell L.	The Bull of Minos	Pan Books	1955
3	Doblhofer E.	Voices in Stone	Granada	1973
4	Evans Sir A.	Palace of Minos	London	1921-35
5	Gordon C.H.	Forgotten Scripts	Ventnor	1968
6	Higgins R.	Minoan and Mycenaean Art	Thames & Hudson	1981
7	Homet M.F.	Son of Suns	Spearman	1963
8	Hood S.	Art in Prehistoric Greece	Pelican	1978
9	King C.	Hieroglyphs to Alphabets	Muller	1977
10	Koutorlis K.	Mycenaean Civilization	Markis	1974
11	Ling R.	The Greek World	Elsevier	1976
12	Luce J.V.	The End of Atlantis	Thames & Hudson	1969
13	Marinatos S.	Crete and Mycenaean Greece	Hirmer	1959
14	Naveh J.	Origins of the Alphabet	Cassell	1975
15	Pope M.	Story of Decipherment	Thames & Hudson	1975

11. Captions

6. Phaistos. Early Palatial Krater *with relief flowers. Imitation of a work in stone and metal. Kamares style. Herakleion Museum.*

10a. Polychrome Vase *with level spout in the Camares style, from the first Palace of Phaistos. c. 1800 B.C. Museum of Herakleion.*

10b. Elliptical Vase. *Polychrome style of Kamares. Old Palace of Phaistos. c. 1800 B.C. Museum of Herakleion.*

18a. An Air View *of* Phaistos.

18b. General view of W. Side. *Messaras Valley in the background.*

19a. Phaistos, *on top of the hill.*

19b. Messara Valley *from Phaistos.*

19c. Ancient ruins below Phaistos.

21. Aghia Galene: *A beautiful resort town near Phaistos.*

23. Spili, a village on the way to Phaistos from Herakleion.

24-25. Matala: *A small village famous for its beach and the numerous little caves.*

28a. Part View of the palace.   *b. Northern Court.*

29. The Little harbour (sidrivani) with the lighthouse in Chania City.

33. Protopalatial *fruitstand painted all-over. Kamares style. Herakleion Museum.*

39. Aghia Fotia: *A beautiful isolated beach on the Southern coast of Crete.*

47. The Village of Sphakia *on the southern coast.*

48. Inscriptions on a rock.

52. Figurine of a Bull, *in bronze from Aghia Triada c. 1500 B.C. Herakleion Museum.*

58. The City of Herakleion.

69. The "Jug of the Reeds" *from Phaistos. Floral style 16th c. B.C.*

70. The Harbour of Herakleion City.

72. Vase *with level spout decorated with foliage. Royal villa, Aghia Triada. c. 1500 B.C. Museum of Herakleion.*

74a. Grand Staircase *of W. Propylon. The Propalatial sanctuary in the foreground.*
   b. West Court with theatrical area and processional Causeway.

78. St. Nicholas *town.*

80. Circular Ritual stores *in the west Courtyard.*

82. Stand of a Clay Object *with dolphins in relief from Phaistos. About the end of M.M. Period.*

83. *Hagia Triada.* Stone Libation *vessel with scenes of boxing. Herakleion Museum.*

84. Corridor of the Magazines.

86a. Central Court.
   b. Pithoi *in the Central Court.*

90. Sanctuary.

92. Storage well.

96. Jug *of the Kamares style from Phaistos 1900-1700 B.C.*

104. Base of a Vase. *Polychrome style of Kamares. Old Palace of Phaistos. 18th Century B.C. Museum of Herakleion.*

106. *Gortyn:* The Temple of Pythios Apollon.

107. *Gortyn:* Odeum.

108-109. Gortyn Code.

114a. Messara plain.
   b. Roofed Rooms *of a Villa.*

115. Stepped Road *to the Villa.*